Keep Looking Up

"Back From The Brink of Death"

The Story of how God Intervened
During a Time of Crisis.

By

David F Hamilton

Copyright © 2017 David F Hamilton

All rights reserved, including the right to reproduce this book, or portions thereof in any form. No part of this text may be reproduced, transmitted, downloaded, decompiled, reverse engineered, or stored, in any form or introduced into any information storage and retrieval system, in any form or by any means, whether electronic or mechanical without the express written permission of the author.

ALL RIGHTS RESERVED.

No part of this book may be reproduced or transmitted in any form or by any means, electronic or mechanical, including photocopying, recording, or by any information storage and retrieval system, without permission in writing from the author, except in the case of brief quotations embodied in reviews.

It is a privilege to introduce you the reader to this book. The story and testimony within these pages communicates the power and message of God; a loving, compassionate, awesome Heavenly Father who hears and answers prayers.

It will grip your heart!

The story as related by Pastor David Hamilton, shows the past, present and future hope of trusting this awesome God. In each page God invades the atmosphere and affects in a supernatural way---24/7 the awareness of His presence. This God is the Alpha (beginning) and Omega (end); but in an intimate way of hopelessness, honesty and reality in trusting in the Word of God (Holy Bible) and His promises one realizes this Heavenly Father cares and is in all the 'wobbly' bits as well.

You will be inspired to keep reading the next page and the next page... An experience of praying like it all depends on God, and to live like it depends on us to keep trusting God against all the odds. You will find what it looks like and feels like in the days and years following this terrible life threatening accident.

I pray that this story and testimony will give you a new courage, new direction, a new willingness to sacrifice everything for knowing the LORD Jesus as your friend on a daily basis.

David Hamilton is a special friend and I honour his integrity and wisdom in sharing "Emma's Story".
Praise the Name of Jesus.

Alan Fenton- Smith

THANKS

Many thanks to all who have encouraged me to write this book about the miracle that saved Emma's life. In particular, to Pam my dear wife and Emma the daughter we nearly lost.

Thank you to all the family as we have shared together in the joys and tears over the years.
Thank you also to our friend Jane Finch who advised me on formatting of this book and also to our dear friend Alan Fenton Smith for his spiritual input and support over the many years.

Contents

                                                               Page

Introduction	9
1. The Dreaded phone Call	12
2. The Power of Prayer	17
3. The Turning Point	25
4. Family Struggles	30
5. Coping with Crisis	36
6. Coming Home	52
7. Back Home	54
8. The Legal Stalkers	60
9. Rehab	66
10. Care Workers at Home	70
11. Be a Fighter	74
12. Emma's own Words	78
13. Twenty Years Later	82

Introduction

The story begins with our daughter Emma being involved in a terrible life threatening accident which left her severely brain damaged. The purpose of this book is that you will be encouraged through the reading of this true story of Emma's miracle especially as you face the many challenges of life.

We cannot even begin to fully understand the mysteries of the Kingdom of God. It requires a life time of discovery through the many facets of life and experiences together with our desire to grow in our faith. Occasionally we get a glimpse or revelation of Gods truth which lifts us to new heights, revealing fresh knowledge and visions of our Lord Jesus Christ who we serve and love. This knowledge of Him causes us to move forward in our faith and understanding.

This journey that I have been called to walk, has had many ups and downs since that moment of asking Jesus into my life.
I can share with you that being a Christian does not exempt us from times of crisis and difficulties; in fact they are often Gods way of doing a deeper work in our lives in order to bring us to a place of maturity and deeper relationship with Him.

JAS 1:2 Consider it pure joy, my brothers, whenever you face trials of many kinds, ³ because you know that the testing of your faith develops perseverance. ⁴ Perseverance must finish its work so that you may be mature and complete, not lacking anything.

I have often been challenged with the question that Jesus put to Peter, "do you love me" and equally the unthinkable situation when Abraham was asked to lay Isaac on the altar.

The ultimate question is this:

"How much are you prepared to give up for me"?

I hope this book will go someway to help us see that the God in whom we serve, the creator of this amazing universe cares and loves us personally and has a plan for our lives. It would be easy to say that we have an all powerful, miracle working God which is true but importantly how is the truth of that applied and worked out through times of crisis, or periods of desperation and confusion.

I do not have all the answers to the unique problems and challenges that we face in life many of which end in tragedy and pain.

Emma's story is still unfolding in her life, molding her as a child of God as the potter forms the clay on the potters wheel.

It is important to remind ourselves that we do not walk it alone, God is with us and he holds all things in His hands, past, present and future.

While we walk this earth, God is shaping us through our faith and obedience in Jesus Christ the savior of the world. He is forming us to reflect the qualities of Jesus, preparing us for heaven and bringing Glory to His name.

It is my belief that the final outcome for our lives is dependent on our willingness to let Jesus be sovereign in our hearts and to also desire His perfect will to be done in our lives every day while we are here on earth.

Isaiah 64:^{8} But now, O LORD, you are our Father; we are the clay, and you are our potter; we are all the work of your hand.

CHAPTER ONE

THE DREADED PHONE CALL

On September 13th 1997 our lives were turned upside down by a phone call, the time was 4.00 a.m. Both my wife Pam and I were awake as it was unusual for our daughter to be out so late. Even our dog Dotty was restless as her nightly routine would be to check all the beds before she settled down, this night Emma's bed was empty. When the phone rang our hearts sank with the fear that it may be some bad news.

It was! Emma had been involved in an accident and had been taken to the Royal United Hospital in Bath We were told to come to the hospital immediately. The nurse would not give any details and sought to assure me that the hospital was running some checks.
I think I went into autopilot we did not want to think the worse and thought maybe it was just a routine observation and hopefully would not be serious. Our two boys Daniel and Simon were sleeping so Pam stayed with them. I would phone her as soon as I could.

On the way to the hospital there was a diversion. I was to find out later that it was the accident that Emma had been involved in which had totally blocked the road, not knowing what the situation was; all I could do was pray;

"Lord let Emma be O.K."

The driver of the car that she was a passenger in had lost control on a bridge, smashing through a wall and hitting a lamp post after rolling over several times. The emergency services were still clearing the road which meant I would need to take a detour to the hospital.

On arrival at the hospital the news was not good. A nurse met me in the foyer and I could see by her face that it was serious. I was told that her checks had included a scan on her brain as she had received a major blow to the head causing internal bleeding. The results were not good and she was to be transferred to Frenchay Hospital Bristol immediately. I was able to see her briefly for a few minutes before she was transferred.

Our once vibrant daughter was now unconscious and had been put into a brace to avoid any movement. Doctors, nurses and ambulance men were busy preparing to move her, every second seem to count. I managed to hold her hand for a few moments; she felt so cold and looked so pale. A friend who saw her at Bristol described her appearance as the nearest to being dead without being dead.

I remember thinking what has happened to my girl who not long ago was all excited about going out with her friends and was so full of life and joy. I was numb with a sense that it had to be a dream, it can't be real, so much confusion, so many thoughts filling my head as her lifeless body was transferred to the ambulance to begin what I hoped was not going to be her last journey from Bath to the Hospital in Bristol.

I followed the ambulance with its blue lights flashing and sirens going, so many times we had watched an ambulance go speeding by and wondered what sad event had taken place. I was not aware that the family were soon to be thrust into a life changing crisis that would last many years.

With all the activity going on I could not speak, part of me was numb, words could not describe the situation adequately but I held on to the hope that Emma would be OK, that her injuries would not be too serious. Making my way to Bristol I remember thinking let this be a horrible dream but I knew it wasn't. The night turned to day and the seriousness of Emma's condition began to unfold.

Arriving at the hospital I was told Emma was being prepared for surgery. Emma spent all morning in surgery we could only wait. By this time, Pam had joined me along with our sons Simon and Daniel. Pam was a real brick, being strong for the boys and trying to keep things as normal as possible .

Emma was placed in Intensive care but by lunchtime she was returned for more surgery due to continued internal bleeding and swelling of the head.

The prognosis was bad. Emma had received a major blow to the right side of the head causing damage to her brain stem and multiple bleeding throughout her brain. Also she had severe bruising to the front left side of her brain caused by her brain rebounding against the inside of her scull following the impact.

A consultant described her injury as being like a dish of blancmange being shaken violently causing the blancmange to split all over. The news could not be worse in terms of a head injury. We were told that the surgeon who would operate on Emma was reputed to be one of the best Neuro Surgeons in the country and that amazingly he happened to be in the hospital when Emma was brought in.

The doctors and consultants could make no promises but would do all they could. We were told later that it was her age of just 18 years that had influenced the medical decision to keep going to give Emma a fighting chance.

It is worth pointing out that when dealing with head injuries no one can determine the final outcome due partly to the complexities of the brain. A small hit on the head can be fatal and yet some can receive a major impact, survive and go on to live a relatively normal life. Our biggest hope was that Emma would survive, that she would have a fighting chance, the doctors and surgeons would do the best they could to make that happen.

"All we could do was hope and pray"

We were told to prepare ourselves for the worse and that even if Emma survived there remained the possibility that she would be severely brain damaged.

Trying to come to terms with the constant flow of bad news was difficult, each time taking us further down to depths of despair. Little did we know that the lives of our family where about to be turned upside down, that Emma was to lose a massive chunk of her life that in the natural could not be replaced and that it would take many years for her life to get back on track.

CHAPTER TWO

THE POWER OF PRAYER

By now the prayer machine of Gods people had swung into action. Our local church met for emergency prayer and soon the local community was praying in our home town of Devizes. Also, Christians in Manchester, Swindon, Southampton, Sheffield and others throughout England had joined the prayer chain. Emma was placed on the internet for prayer and people prayed as far away as Australia and America.

When we finally saw Emma she was almost unrecognizable. Our hearts sank as we stood by her bed observing the monitors and tubes that were attached to her body. Her face was so badly swollen and her head had been bandaged up as the surgeons had taken away half of her scull which had been shattered by the impact. I was told later that this was done to enable the brain to swell for the purpose to allow as much blood flow to reach the bruised and damaged parts of her brain.

The pain and grief we felt was unbearable. We were aware of the many prayers being said for Emma and never gave up hope that God would intervene. We felt like bystanders in an unfolding drama that was totally out of our control.

We prayed "Lord give Emma her life" we could pray nothing more. Yet deep inside I was beginning to feel a sense of anger towards God. Thoughts crowded in such as "How can you let this happen" and if she was the only Christian in the car, "How come she's the only one injured and fighting for her life" I mean isn't God meant to watch over his children.

Annie a leader with me at the church asked, "How can we pray"? I said, "pray for a miracle" because that is what she needed.

At times, I could not speak because of the pain and trauma I was feeling. I rang my sister Kit and her husband John from the hospital to tell her the bad news when she answered the phone I could get no words out, I was dumb, I could hear her voice but I was speechless, I moved my lips but no sound came out.
They dropped everything at their home in Crowborough Sussex and came to the hospital to support us, I wasn't very good company, we were in a state of shock.
I remember my sister's words "She is going to be OK" Words of encouragement and hope but I was still numb with shock.

For twenty-four hours there was no sign of life, our hearts were breaking and I felt like running from God and the call on my life. We had committed our lives to serving the Lord but I thought "Lord I don't want to get behind a pulpit again" I thought to myself "this was not part of the deal" as if serving God could be described as a deal.

We had faced a few challenges in the past and this seemed like the final straw.

But God was dealing with my own life, I know that sounds weird. I knew I could not pretend with God. Either I believed in Him and His Word, which reveals his healing power and his promises. Either I was prepared to apply what I believed to be true to the situation we were facing or the past thirty years of my life was just a sham. Yes, I had taught on trusting Jesus for every need, believing in His sovereignty and ability to heal through faith. I had taught on taking up our cross and following Jesus and had laid hands in the sick.

I had preached on knowing His strength during the storms of life and to hold on to the promises of God and that nothing was impossible for Him.

2 Corinthians 1[20] For all the promises of God find their Yes in him. That is why it is through him that we utter our Amen to God for his glory.

I had preached on the need to make Jesus Lord of our lives and knowing Him to be our number one priority. I had made Christ central to the future of our family and trusted in God for their well being. I had come to understand the importance of humility and dependency on our God. I have recognized my short comings and was aware that I am far from perfect but have always believed that we are accepted in His grace and forgiven.

Both Pam and I had dedicated our lives to serve the Lord and obey His calling and direction in our walk and service. I had prayed for the sick and believed in the miraculous and seen many answers to prayer. Now all of this was being condensed into our very own crisis.

I was beginning to learn that faith without works is dead.

Mark 10^{27} Jesus looked at them and said, "With man it is impossible, but not with God. For all things are possible with God."

Something was happening in my own life while Emma lay in a coma.
Deep down I knew that what ever happened to Emma, I had no choice in terms of serving the Lord. In my heart, I knew that even my daughter could not be more important then obeying Gods call on my life. That almost sounds heartless as I write. After all, our children are the apple of our eye, they are Gods gift to us, and all we have belongs to Him including our children.

There is a point, a crossroad in our lives, a crisis point where we have to let go and lay everything on the altar like when Abraham laid Isaac on the altar. I am not talking about going through some religious ritual or offering lip service through some shallow prayer.

No, this is where the rubber hits the road and you have to decide to choose the narrow road of sacrifice where carrying baggage is not an option. This is where you go to the back of the queue metaphorically and put others and God before your greatest need. Where humility takes over and you become a servant, where your will is subordinated to Gods will and you become receptive for the Holy Spirit to have dominion in your life. Where you pray in all sincerity as Jesus did at Gethsemane.

Matthew 26:39 *And going a little farther he fell on his face and prayed, saying, "My Father, if it be possible, let this cup pass from me; nevertheless, not as I will, but as you will."*

This is the point in your journey when you change from being a disciple or servant of Jesus to being His friend.

John 15:15 *No longer do I call you servants, for the servant does not know what his master is doing; but I have called you friends, for all that I have heard from my Father I have made known to you.*

I had taught on Matthew 7:12-14 where we see the two options for life The Narrow way or the wide way.
His rule and dominion is not about discussion it's about our walk, our desire to live, work and serve according to the principles of the Kingdom. Jesus presents us with the two choices. Two options with no in between, no sitting on that painful fence.

Gate 1: Wide = The world = Easy option = Leads to destruction.

Gate 2: Narrow = The kingdom of God = Difficult option = Life.

God was dealing with a part of my life that no head knowledge or degree in doctrine could teach me. I was about to learn what it would really mean to lay down my life and die to self.

The following passage reveals much about the price we pay to follow Jesus:

*Luke 9:57 As they were going along the road, someone said to him, "I will follow you wherever you go." ⁵⁸And Jesus said to him, "Foxes have holes, and birds of the air have nests, but the Son of Man has nowhere to lay his head." ⁵⁹To another he said, "Follow me." But he said, "Lord, let me first go and **bury** my father."⁶⁰And Jesus said to him, "Leave the dead to bury their own dead. But as for you, go and proclaim the kingdom of God."⁶¹Yet another said, "I will follow you, Lord, but let me first say farewell to those at my home."⁶²Jesus said to him, "No one who puts his hand to the plough and looks back is fit for the kingdom of God."*

Jesus always responded out of love and compassion but never out of sentimentality. His purpose and commission was always at the forefront of His ministry and decisions.

Remember when at the age of twelve his mother and earthly father were worried about where he was. The scriptures tell us of his response.

Luke 2:49 *And he said to them, "Why were you looking for me? Did you not know that I must be in my Father's house?"*

Much of life is about our choices we make and with our choices come the responsibility for those choices. We choose to love and we choose to hate, we choose to obey or choose to do our own thing. We choose to follow Christ or we choose to go our own way. We choose to apply Gods Word to our lives or we choose to conform to the pattern of this world. Many try to find a middle road but God does not give us that option.

To choose life is to believe in the giver of life, he is Lord of all or not Lord at all.

Deut 30:19 *I call heaven and earth to witness against you today, that I have set before you life and death, blessing and curse. Therefore choose life, that you and your offspring may live.*

The narrow gate is too narrow to take a lot of baggage. The challenge is to lay it down. Future expectations, self, the way of the world and the desire for wealth. Our own ego, our own so called rights, they all need laying down, because when you are on a long journey you best travel light.

You must pass through on your own. It is personal and requires individual response. Jesus does not give us the option of allowing someone else to make the decision for us. I spent the first part of my life following the crowds trying to be what I thought people wanted me to be, I wanted to be accepted and not rejected, big mistake.

But I found my identity in Christ and I was set free. I discovered that God accepts us as we are and then He begins to change us from the inside out.

2 Corinthians 3^{18} And we all, with unveiled face, beholding the glory of the Lord, are being transformed into the same image from one degree of glory to another. For this comes from the Lord who is the Spirit.

You must be ready to face challenges, persecution, isolation, hardship and sufferings all guaranteed on the narrow way. I knew all this because I had read it and taught it, but I was about to learn what this really means as we were faced with the possibility of losing our beautiful precious daughter.

CHAPTER THREE

THE TURNING POINT

Eventually after many tears and much soul searching. I came to a place in my heart where I knew whatever happened to Emma I would continue to follow the Lord. I knew I had no choice, much of what happens in life is about our choices and our choices always carry consequences like our choice to rebel against God. But when God calls you, when Jesus saves you; when the heart of Jesus touches your heart, you can never be the same again. Once He has illuminated your life and lifted you up from a corrupt and sinful life you can never return to that sub-standard life of darkness and deceit. The following verse tells us who we are and where we are in Christ.

1 Peter 2^9 But you are a chosen race, a royal priesthood, a holy nation, a people for his own possession, that you may proclaim the excellencies of him who called you out of darkness into his marvellous light.

It seems this was the turning point for God to start healing Emma. Perhaps what was happening to Emma was part of a bigger picture. Our pain was still unbearable the sense of numbness and grief weighed heavily upon us but after twenty-four hours the hopelessness was being replaced with hope.

My anger and confusion was being replaced with faith and it was then that we saw the first sign of life. Her hands had begun to take on the appearance of Palsy an indication of paralysis and as we looked at her lifeless body we noticed something which caused our doubting hearts to move into a living faith.

Emma's little finger moved.

MT 17:20 *He replied, "Because you have so little faith. I tell you the truth, if you have faith as small as a mustard seed, you can say to this mountain, `Move from here to there' and it will move. Nothing will be impossible for you.*

This was for us like the mustard seed. The nurses and doctors told us not to get our hopes up to high. **"What"** was our response, "but there is life, her brain is working", God is at work.

The miracle had begun.

Whenever we pray for someone who is near to death we pray believing that there is a spiritual connection with the Holy Spirit. We believe there is a bypassing of the natural senses although I understand the hearing is the last remaining sense to go.

So we believed God could minister to her inner most being, that body, soul and spirit would come into harmony for the healing process to begin. This is how God created us to be, for our bodies and our soul to be subordinate to our spirit. The new birth process is a rebirth of the spirit that submits to the sovereignty and divinity of the Holy Spirit, who leads us, guides us and helps us.

Romans 8:^{14} For all who are led by the Spirit of God are sons of God.

We began to sing songs of thanksgiving over her life, praise to almighty God. I would joke if anything would bring her out of this coma my singing would. It did not matter if people thought we were crazy, we had passed the self-conscious stage. God was in the house and the atmosphere in the hospital was being charged with the impartation of faith and lives were beginning to be affected by Gods presence.

In the book of Job we read :

Job 37:4 -5 God's majestic voice thunders his commands, creating miracles too marvellous for us to understand.

How can we articulate how God works, His ways are way beyond our limited understanding. Have you noticed how we like to put God in a box and dictate to Him what and how He should do things?

Remember the story of Lazarus who had been dead for four days. Martha told Jesus that had he come earlier things would be different. Jesus does not operate under the dictates of mankind; he had another outcome in mind which would give glory to God.

John11:4 *But when Jesus heard it he said, "This illness does not lead to death. It is for the glory of God, so that the Son of God may be glorified through it."*

I think we can go through life scratching the surface of Gods heart, doing our bit, fitting him around our plans and kidding ourselves we are somewhere we are not. But it is only when God shines the torchlight of His Truth into our hearts and reveals our true condition that we are then faced with the reality of embracing the truth or denying it.

Now it is the embracing of the truth which will lead to sacrifice. It is a fork in the road and the direction we take will determine our destiny.

Fundamentally there is no choice, for to deny His truth is to live a life of deception which will lead to death. We cannot pretend with God. He gave the most precious most valuable person in His life, His only begotten Son, that we might have life.

John 3:16 *"For God so loved the world, that he gave his only Son, that whoever believes in him should not perish but have eternal life.*

Can we really stand before the creator of all things and say "you can have this much of my life but no more, you can have so many hours a week but no more". I cannot stress this enough, God was looking for me to lay everything on the altar and I was beginning to learn what it really meant to die to self. A new chapter was beginning in my life as well as Emma's.

John 12:24 Truly, truly, I say to you, unless a grain of wheat falls into the earth and dies, it remains alone; but if it dies, it bears much fruit.

CHAPTER FOUR

FAMILY STRUGGLES

The effects on the family were enormous; I guess we all handle things in different ways. Simon was angry with the driver who had caused the accident; he was only sixteen years of age and wanted revenge for the drunk driver who nearly took Emma's life. Daniel who was fourteen at the time said very little, but exercised a quiet inner strength; we all deal with things in different ways.

Pam was brilliant she had to be strong and be there for the boys and we agreed that I would stay at the hospital until we could sort things out. Pam returned home to find many flowers from friends' family and strangers, it seemed the whole community had taken Emma to there heart, this was a great comfort to us all.

Often Pam's mum and dad would stay with the boys while Pam could be at the hospital with me. Their hearts were breaking also with the effect of the situation taking its toll on their health. Sadly, Pam's dad was to die of a aneurism four months later but not before he had witnessed Emma's dramatic healing.

I barely left Emma's side continuing to pray, sing, read the bible and talk to her knowing that as a child of God her spirit was alive and active even though she was being kept alive by a machine.

I guess if I was honest it was being there with Emma that somehow gave me strength to cope. That almost sounds selfish but Emma was fighting for her life and I wanted to fight with her, I knew I wasn't much use but it just didn't seem right to be somewhere else while Emma lay in a coma in intensive care.

If I could I would have changed places with her as I am sure any parent would do the same for their child. There was I believe, a battle in heaven being fought for Emma's life, a precious child of God. I had passed through the fire of my own limitations and I knew now that God had begun an amazing work.

Eph 3:16 I pray that out of his glorious riches he may strengthen you with power through his Spirit in your inner being,

The church at Devizes where great, releasing me from pastoral duties to concentrate on being with Emma. Our brothers and sisters in the Lord stood with us in fervent and persistent prayer. I was to learn that when God is present in situations and lives, then those around are effected and influenced by what God is doing. His invisible presence begins to touch lives in an unexplainable but tangible way.

God invades the atmosphere when faith is released changing the hopelessness of a faithless environment into hope and joy. Receptive hearts are affected and changed.

Encouragement is released breaking through the discouragement and despair; joy begins to lift the heavy heart, tears of healing start to flow.

This is heaven touching earth.

That which is natural becomes influenced by Gods rule and truth. Body and soul become subordinate to the spiritual. This I believe was a glimpse of how God intended life to exist in the beginning when He created all things. Occasionally God allows the light to shine ever brighter bringing deeper revelation of His life and His kingdom rule. It is the point of revelation that impacts the hearts of people, not through intellect or reason but purely a glimpse into a kingdom that eventually becomes your home, your dwelling place, the place you pitch your tent. It is that place where the theories become reality, where boundaries become unlimited.

1 Chronicles 4:10 Jabez called upon the God of Israel, saying, "Oh that you would bless me and enlarge my border, and that your hand might be with me, and that you would keep me from harm so that it might not bring me pain!" And God granted what he asked.

Prayer:
Lord may our faith be enlarged to see beyond the limitations of my understanding to grasp the bigger picture of your Kingdom here on earth. Help me not to be content with a superficial existence that only has it's anchor in my needs. Let the eyes of my heart be opened that I might see all the possibilities for my life in Christ my savior and Lord, my spiritual ears to hear your voice and my will to be laid on the altar of sacrifice to do your will. Amen

1 Cor 13: [9] *For we know in part and we prophesy in part,* [10]*but when the perfect comes, the partial will pass away.* [11]*When I was a child, I spoke like a child, I thought like a child, I reasoned like a child. When I became a man, I gave up childish ways.* [12]*For now we see in a mirror dimly, but then face to face. Now I know in part; then I shall know fully, even as I have been fully known.* [13]*So now faith, hope, and love abide, these three; but the greatest of these is love.*

A hospital worker came to me as I was reading the bible to Emma, this was her comment:
"I have been walking these wards for two years praying silently in my own words and in tongues but this is the first time I have seen God move like this, I am so encouraged".

The wife of a man who had a stroke was there with her family, she asked me how Emma was doing. She was still in a coma but I said "God is continuing to heal her" she fell into my arms and wept, tears of release. No words were necessary, God does things His way. Her family cried too as they saw her letting go of her pain. I don't know if her husband recovered but I prayed at his bedside and left him the book "Apostle of faith" by Smith Wigglesworth. I hope he got chance to read it.

I remember asking a nurse "what church did you say you went to", "I didn't" she said "but I'm going to find one" was her reply. She then told me that several years previous she had lost her brother in a road accident and had become bitter and angry with God and had stopped going to church. "But" she said "I am going back".

I stood amazed as God ministered to people's hearts, His grace was flowing, and restoration of lives was in progress.

A woman whose son had been hit over the head with a crowbar and left for dead for several hours in an isolated area began to believe for her son to recover. We watched her fear turn to hope; her pain etched face slowly over time began to change to one of a peaceful countenance. Another personal tragedy that hopefully had a happy ending.

Emma's recovery was so rapid that it surprised the medical staff.
They were brilliant. I would say to them "With your expertise and Gods healing power you make a great team"

Emma remained in a coma for Eight days. During that time we would read to her from the bible the following scripture over and over believing she could hear every word.

Romans 8:37-39. *In all these things we are more than conquerors through him who loved us. For I am convinced that neither death nor life, neither angels nor demons, neither the present nor the future, nor any powers, neither height nor depth, nor anything else in all creation, will be able to separate us from the love of God that is in Christ Jesus our Lord.*

There's something about speaking out the declarations of Gods Word, like replacing the negatives in this world with Gods truth. It's the power of agreement (Matthew 18:19) and we are reminded that all His promises are Yes and Amen. (2 Corinthians 1:20)

We thank God for Emma's life and healing. We thank God for our two sons Simon and Daniel each one being equally a precious gift to us that make up our close family, each one dealing with the issues in their own way, we thank God for helping us all cope during a time of major crisis.

CHAPTER FIVE

COPING WITH CRISIS

I had always thought that when someone came out from a coma that it was a very peaceful and joyful event. Well it was indescribably joyful but very far from being peaceful. The consultant had told us previously that when she came out of the coma they wanted her to come out kicking, screaming and fighting and that is exactly what happened.
She had no control over her body movements or what she said, in fact she used words that I didn't think she knew and I certainly won't repeat them.

Often the nurses were screamed at and at one point I got a hefty slap on the face. I was later to find that she had no idea who I was during her time in hospital. Her arms and legs were flying every where and anything that was attached to her like tubes, catheters and oxygen masks were quickly dispatched.

Eight days of silence was replaced with unprepared chaos and the need for constant care and attention.
She was a danger to herself especially as the surgeons had taken away half of her scull away which had been shattered by the impact, one knock on the head or a fall out of bed would have been fatal. During her coma Emma contracted pneumonia

and was placed on a cooling mattress to keep the fever under control, this went on for days but eventually the fever broke.

The Hospital was great and provided Pam and I accommodation for the first week so we could spend time at Emma's bedside and it meant we were close at hand if needed. The first few days we would lay there wondering if the phone would ring with bad news. Sometimes, unable to sleep, I would stand in the corridor of the hospital in the early hours of the morning, and see the less fortunate ones being wheeled out under covers.

I would pray Lord don't let Emma be another statistic, a lifeless corpse on a mortuary slab. I could not help but be saddened by the steady stream of lives being lost by accidents or illness. Each one carrying their own story of heartache grief and pain.

Life is so precious, we know not what tomorrow will bring but Jesus encourages us to not worry. The word worry means to fret or torment oneself with or suffer from disturbing thoughts but Jesus, whose teaching was not only spiritual and profound but also very down to earth taught us this:

MT 6:34 *"Do not worry about tomorrow, for tomorrow will worry about itself. Each day has enough trouble of its own".*

He also reminds us that he is the only true source of peace and rest. I was still learning these basic principles and discovering how hard it is to let go and trust in God for everything.

Mat 11:28 If you are tired from carrying heavy burdens, come to me and I will give you rest.

During the first days the pain was so great, I just couldn't bear the thought of losing our daughter. I would have these flashes of me standing at her funeral watching her coffin being lowered into the ground, it seemed so real and the tears would start to flow, I would then snap out of it with the relief of knowing it was only my imagination.
In situations like this I guess the mind can become a real battleground between faith and fear.

We discover a lot about ourselves when we are faced with crisis. Our weaknesses, our true level of faith, where we really put our trust and hope, what our real priorities are. I have learned that we often pay lip service to a lot of things not least our belief and trust in God.

But when your faith is tested in a real-life crisis then it will go one of two ways, you will either run away from God and I wanted to run or your faith will be strengthened through the fire and you will come through stronger and better for it.

1 Peter 1:^{7} so that the tested genuineness of your faith---more precious than gold that perishes though it is tested by fire--- may be found to result in praise and glory and honour at the revelation of Jesus Christ.

We will never know what we can endure until we have

faced the storms of life. We may be good at preaching and expounding on the word of God or be an expert on the art of survival but the experience of coping and suffering through crisis will sharpen your perspective renewing your priorities on life and bring a new dimension to your walk and ministry with God.

I have often prayed "Lord thank you for the truths and lessens you have shown me through the trials of life, but please, please Lord, help me to learn the easy way because the hard way seems to be so painful". Faith can be contagious as in times of revival and it seemed that alongside us in similar situations were others who started to believe for a miracle for their loved ones. When God invades an environment or situation then you become conscious of His presence and activity and yet you become almost detached from what is happening. You can only stand back and watch the miracle of His intervention unfold.
The atmosphere changes and it affects both believers and non-believers in a super natural way. Perhaps this is what happens when revival breaks out.

As I witnessed Gods hand at work I felt any contribution of my own was not only not needed, but would probably hinder what God was doing. All I could do was stand in awe and wonder at His amazing miraculous love, grace and healing. Like an open window into heaven, His kingdom coming to earth releasing His will and revealing His glory.

Emma's recovery was rapid and astounded the doctors. She was still very vulnerable and needed round the clock care. She was moved to a high dependency unit and was now able to breath without a machine. This was a great relief as no one knew what would happen until the machine was turned off.

She was unable to swallow and she had had a tracheotomy to enable her to breath, she still bears the scar today. The last eight days had turned our lives upside down. We were faced with a situation that was totally out of our control, and when you don't have control, life can go a bit wobbly but it is then that you realize how much you need Gods help.

As a Pastor I find it is during the times like bereavement and crisis that people are most open to the truth of Gods Word.
Well here we were trusting in God like never before, I had preached it, taught it but never been faced with the reality quite like this.

This crisis was to be the beginning of an eight year roller coaster ride that was to see Emma not just fighting for her life but also having to rebuild and rediscover her life. We don't prepare ourselves for much of what happens in life, a bit like having children we learn and make our adjustments in the course of the journey, making mistakes along the way.

But this I know that when we live by faith and follow Christ Jesus there is an equipping on our lives that will enable us to overcome the trails of life in a way that turns a negative situation into a positive one. In so doing we are able to be a tremendous witness for God as He helps us to overcome.

***Philippians 4**:^13 I can do all things through him who strengthens me.*

Crisis's come in all shapes and sizes and they are normal to life and we don't have to pretend that we are coping when we aren't. I believe a primary attitude for overcoming the storms of life is being real and honest with our self, each other and God.

The medical way of dealing with many problems is to prescribe medication like anti-depressants or refer you to some therapist. This may have some value but I believe the biggest value above anything else is when you put your hand and life in the hands of the savior of the world and trust in Him.

You must believe who you are in Christ, and learn to understand the bigger picture. He can do more then we can imagine. He is a supernatural God, who can not only transform, heal and restore but also bring good out of something bad.

We don't always see the purpose or strategy of God at the time, who would have thought that what Joseph went through in Egypt was to be the means to save a nation or the persecution in the early church was to be the means to see the Gospel spread throughout the world. When Jesus went through His crisis and lets be real about this it was a crisis, firstly he gave up his life, laid it down, endured the mockery and pain, He knew the final sacrifice was to not just die but die a painful humiliating death.

But He also knew the bigger picture when he cried out in the garden of Gethsemane.

"Father, if you are willing, take this cup from me; yet not my will, but yours be done."

He knew his death and subsequent resurrection would alter the course of history by establishing his church, defeating the devil and sealing the new covenant with his blood. A new covenant that has brought hope, healing and salvation to multitudes of people from all walks of life.

In Matthews Gospel chapter four we see that Jesus faced a crisis as the devil tempted Him, each time Jesus quoted scripture, He was quoting the truth and neutralized the devils tactics of temptation and deceit.

God's word is truly a powerful weapon against the deceptive strategies and lies of the devil.

I don't know why some who have faced similar injuries as Emma like our nephew Andrew don't survive, or why some get healed of terminal illnesses and some don't.

I can only write what was our experience. It seems that every situation is unique and God speaks uniquely to us all as the factors of the situations we face come together.
There seems to be many things that happen in life that catch us unawares and we are seldom prepared for the unexpected traumas of life. They are moments when God gets our

unequivocal attention; it is the time when our faith becomes action, and the honesty of our hearts are questioned and challenged.

Jesus asked Peter three times if he loved Him, each time he said yes. *John 21:15.*
Is there any limit to our love for Him? Is our love unconditional?
Where on the scale of life do we say:

"hang on God this was not part of the deal"

God has made us with feelings and emotions but also He created us to be spiritual beings who are led by the Holy Spirit. This does not mean we become robots with suppressed feelings; it means that with the help of the Holy Spirit we are becoming complete in Christ and in so doing are fashioned and shaped to deal with life according to the principles of the Kingdom of God which is truth.
I speak these things not to fill up a page but to share the importance of letting go of a sub standard faithless life and trusting in our God for every situation.

The rich young man in the gospel of Matthew Chapter 19 went away sad because he failed to let go of his legalistic, and "salvation through works" attitude. Jesus challenged his heart condition which created a crisis for him.

The ultimate challenge is this:

"Is God more important then my wealth and security, more important then the kingdom I am building for my life, more important then my family, (that's a tough one)"
The amazing truth is that God loves us as a Father loves His child and wants the best for our lives. He will provide all our needs according to His riches in Glory.

Philippians 4:19 And my God will supply every need of yours according to his riches in glory in Christ Jesus.

As we live by faith He is glorified through our lives. He longs that we trust him in all circumstances, he is so faithful.

We only see in part but God sees the beginning to the end requiring us to trust in Him for the future.

The prognosis for Emma was uncertain as is the case for head injuries but judging by past cases of those with similar injuries, we were told that if she survived she may be in a vegetative state unable to walk and lead a normal life. My mind became a blur, the pain so great I could not function. These are the experts, in the natural, things looked pretty grim to say the least. If only I could swap places with Emma I thought, after all I've had a pretty good life, but for Emma life was just beginning.
  She had just finished college and was ready to step into the big wide world, she had her dreams and plans, she was full of life, beautiful with her whole life before her.

After four weeks Emma was losing weight rapidly due to her inability to swallow, she was getting quite frail and weak. I would try to stimulate her brain with music, pictures and drawing which she had always loved, she grabbed the pencil done a sketch of my face. The first attempt was equivalent to an eight or nine year old and needless to say pretty ugly. Two weeks later the improvement was amazing, she actually made me look quite handsome, another miracle.

The consultant explained that her brain was a bit like a filing cabinet that had been tipped out and gradually every file had to be replaced back into its right place and that this will take a long time.

The nurse came to me and told me that due to her weight loss Emma would need to be force fed due to her inability to swallow and would I help. She explained the process which was not very pleasant. This required four people holding her down while the nurse inserted a feeding tube up her nose and down into her stomach. The high energy liquid food was then poured into a funnel connected to the tube. I will never forget the look on Emma's face as she went through this ordeal. She looked at me as if to say "help me" in her confused state. At one time I could bear it no more and promptly left to go outside, my heart breaking, tears flowing, asking Gods help to strengthen me.

Up to this point Emma had no understanding of what was happening. In her confused mind I was a stranger and the hospital was a prison somewhere in France. She believed that she had committed a terrible crime and that the police were continually turning up to question her. She was so full of fear and would cry in desperation, I would try to reassure her but it was often futile.

She was transferred to The Royal United hospital in Bath which made it easier for friends and family to visit. I was told I could sleep by the side of her bed.
We had been so blessed with the generosity and love of everyone who came and supported us with gifts of homemade cakes, encouragement and prayer.

The journey was continuing and we were convinced that there would be a happy ending, what we didn't realize was that the journey would take several years and for Emma it is still continuing.

Emma before the accident

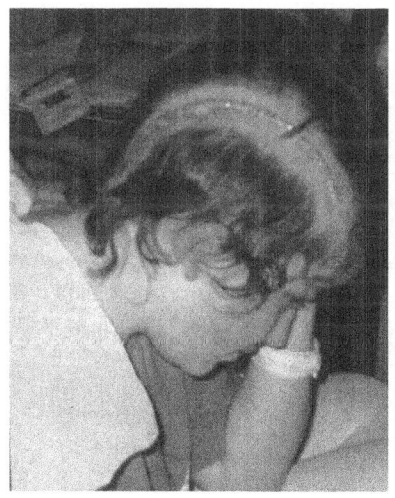

Emma after being in a coma

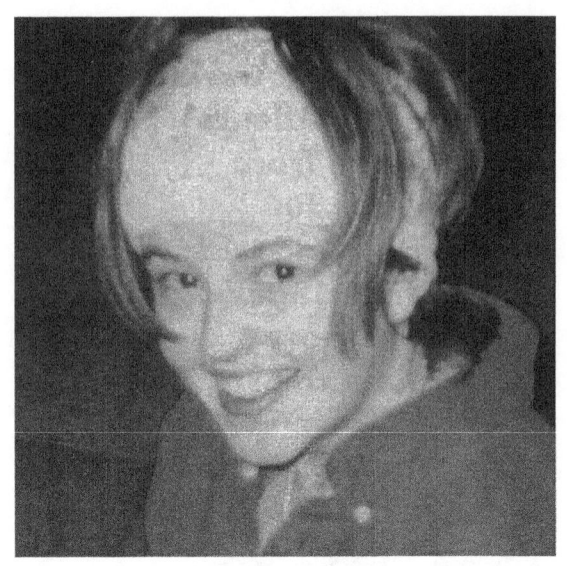

After operation to have part of scull put back

Emma sharing her story at a church.

A recent photo

With her family left to right Emma, Danny, Mum Simon, Nan and Dad

Emma's Sketch of her dad done at 3 weeks after her accident and 2 weeks later which reveals the amazing speed of Emma's recovery.

Emma 8 years after accident

CHAPTER SIX

COMING HOME

Her rapid recovery continued and with great joy we were told Emma could come home for a weekend after a total of Five weeks in hospital, this in itself is incredible, we had been told it would be many months at least. They wanted to see how we would cope. We were so excited; the wheelchair that was provided was never used except by our two sons who thought it was a great opportunity to see how fast they could go in it.

We will never fully know the way God has blessed and encouraged people through Emma's miracle but it goes on today. We would take Emma to visit the many churches that had prayed for Emma, she wanted to thank them but also it was such an encouragement to the many who had prayed, to see this miracle first hand bringing Glory to God.

Emma had to fight the fight of her life, her strength, faith and determination has helped her to be where she is today.

What ever you face in life do not give up, turn it around for Gods glory, it won't always be easy but that is part of the process of making you who and what you are today.
Don't try to do it on your own; if you do you will probably fail.

Matt 11:29 Take my yoke upon you and learn from me, for I am gentle and humble in heart, and you will find rest for your souls.

Remember its not just about you, it's about what God wants to do through you. For that to happen effectively you must be humble and filled with the Holy Spirit for this is the provision of empowerment on your life.

Acts 13:52 And the disciples were filled with joy and with the Holy Spirit.

Don't say that this is for someone else; if you are a child of God then the gift of the Holy Spirit is for you to be led by and use the authority he has given you. You can put that robber and thief the devil where he belongs under you feet. Speak out the promises of God for your life and reject the negative words and thoughts that crowd in from unbelief and doubt.

Rom 8:39 In all these things we are more than conquerors through him who loved us.

CHAPTER SEVEN

BACK HOME

We had been in unchartered territory for five weeks and now, what was a miracle in itself, we were back home. We could hardly contain our excitement. In just five weeks and we could see Emma improving almost daily. The weekend went well with even a trip into our town of Devizes in Wiltshire.

Many people knew Emma and probably read of Emma's accident in the local paper. They were amazed to see Emma walking with Pam albeit slowly and cautiously. The marathon trip would normally take about five minutes to get to the town centre, but on this momentous occasion it took best part of 45 minutes partly due to her fragile condition and the many who stopped in amazement to speak to Pam and Emma. The churches had been praying for Emma and the local paper had run a front page news item on Emma's accident titled:

"Teenager fights for life after car crash"

So it was somewhat understandable that people were amazed to see her in town so soon, not in a wheelchair or with crutches but walking. Some had even thought she had died.

A follow up article headline on October 23rd 1997 read:

"Emma back home after miraculous recovery".

In just twelve days Emma had progressed from not walking, not talking and not eating to coming home. This was indeed a miracle.

Later in Emma's recovery major secular magazines such as Woman and Company were to publish Emma's story.

She had not yet had the side of her scull put back so the hospital had provided her with a purpose-built helmet that resembled a horse riding helmet. Emma would decorate it with various hats to conceal it, the helmet did a great job in protecting her from any falls or bumps, her balance was very poor she was vulnerable and still quite frail.

The decision for Emma to come home permanently was as much based on our ability to cope as Emma's safety and recovery but by Monday the hospital agreed to let Emma stay at home much to our relief.
The story so far had been of rapid and miraculous healing of which we continually thanked God. On one of her hospital check ups that were to follow, one of the consultants looked at her, asked her to walk up and down.
Emma smiled with a sense of achievement as well as being the centre of attention. After a period of prolonged silence the consultant with a look that resembled an artist surveying his work said the words that we would never forget:

"I think there has been another source at work here".

We knew that source to be the healing power of prayer through Jesus Christ. Isn't it fantastic when even the specialists recognize a divine work, it sort of demolishes the arguments of the skeptics.

On another visit to have her scull put back, the doctor arrived with her notes a young doctor from New Zealand. After looking at Emma and the notes he replied:

"I think I have the wrong notes"

He continued briefly looking around the ward for the real Emma Hamilton but he was right first time.

I remember when God spoke to me in the hospital He impressed on my heart that He would heal her 98% but it would be the other 2% that would give Him the glory. I didn't understand this and some even suggested this was a lack of faith on my part. Our prayer at the beginning was give Emma her life so 98% was more then we could have hoped for. Pam wasn't sure what would be worse, Emma dying or being in a vegetative state and permanently handicapped. Like myself, Pam had to settle the issues; she would accept the outcome and trust in God. Praise God the outcome was very far from the original prognosis.

Let me tell you about the 2%.

Emma was still fundamentally the daughter we had always known and loved but her brain injury had robbed her of her confidence and self assurance, it was as if she had lost something of her old self. It was as if we were grieving this loss and yet physically she was still with us.

She had lost much of her short term and long term memory; which thankfully was to return in time. She would struggle with coping with situations and what we would call normal relational behavior. Minor incidents would seem like a major crisis, which often would create stress for all concerned. Her fatigue levels were very low causing her to need sleep every few hours. A short walk with Dotty our dog would be enough to drain her of her energy.

She would often have mood swings that was difficult for all the family to deal with including Emma.
Her behavior could swing from being quite child like, to a normal teenager. She would wave and shout to strangers from her window lacking some of her normal social boundaries.

For seven years life was like a roller coaster. Good days and bad days, outbursts of anger, times of not speaking, false accusations and frustration and yet within a few hours it was as if nothing had happened.

As previously stated, we are very seldom prepared for the unexpected in life but I can honestly say that our faith in Jesus

Christ gave us an inner strength; His peace would fill our hearts during the storms.

There is always a bigger picture.

The challenge is to draw on the heavenly resources that God has promised, to not dwell on the negatives of "may be" and "what-ifs". At times I would find myself thinking, how her life would be now if she had not had the accident.
I would imagine her forging a successful life, enjoying every moment, surrounded by friends. She was going for it and she had the character and determination to fulfill her dreams.

As I entertained these thoughts the clouds would gather and I would have to shake myself to thank God for her life a precious life, still with us and still fighting. Slowly that same character and determination was returning which I believe helped her enormously in her recovery.

After a couple of years she tried to go back to work but it proved to be too early resulting in extreme fatigue and stress. It was a set back for Emma who was so determined to get back to a normal life, but we were all learning that her journey of recovery was going to be a long road. The doctor at the time had very little understanding in head injuries and promptly prescribed her anti depressants and told her he did not give sick notes to healthy people. I was amazed at the lack of knowledge and inability to differ between a psychological problem like depression and a neurological injury. If that is true for a doctor then we can see how difficult it is for the average person who has had no training in these areas.

As we fail to understand the deep complexities of head injuries we are inclined to label the sufferer as crazy, mental or just plain weird.

This effects friendships and relationships with those being closest being affected most. When we don't understand something or feel threatened by something or someone then our natural response is often to back away and then blame someone else for our actions.

CHAPTER EIGHT

LEGAL STALKERS

While Emma was in hospital I had a call from a good Christian friend who happened to be a solicitor who specialized in civil claims. She explained to me that Emma would probably be eligible for compensation from the insurers of the Hire car company of the vehicle that Emma was travelling in.

The driver had been over the drink drive limit. He was subsequently found guilty and was banned from driving for fifteen months and issued with a fine of £500 plus prosecution costs. Emma's condition was not discussed during the driver's court case even though his actions had nearly killed her.

Emma was given access to some of the best consultants and specialists in the country. Where we were living in Wiltshire, we received very little follow up help with both the Social services and mental health department refusing to accept responsibility for Emma.

The Insurers had accepted liability and so it was up to the solicitors to agree on a suitable package of compensation for her injuries that would take into account her ability to work and her quality of life in the future and potential care needs. Whilst this was in part a blessing and indeed I believe Gods provision for Emma's many needs. It was also the source of great stress that had a major bearing on Emma's recovery.

Her life was not her own, everything became driven by appointments with various experts all over the country. She was frequently followed and filmed not knowing until a copy of the video would come through the door. Once their cover was blown they would very quickly beat a hasty retreat.

Not only was it difficult enough to deal with the massive change on her life but she also had to cope with what she referred to as her "legal stalkers".

Now if this was designed partly to force Emma into an out of court settlement their attempts were futile. Being the fighter she is, she became even more determined to see it through. We did not realize at the time that this fight was to last for over seven years.

Our solicitor had told us it could go all the way to the court steps, well it went all the way to the court doors in Bristol Crown Court where thankfully she was offered a settlement that would provide an adequate income for her to live a normal life. The settlement was both satisfactory to Emma and the insurers legal team.

She could now get on with rebuilding her life with some degree of financial security. I know now that although it was a tough seven year legal battle, Emma now has a quality of life and a standard of living that would not have been possible without it.

The use of cameramen and private detectives are used for the insurers to build a case for reduced compensation. They would frequently follow Emma, a perfectly legal practice that was designed to discredit her claim and counteract the claims of the specialists on Emma's legal team.

This I believe had a counter productive effect on Emma's recovery even driving Emma to suicidal thoughts at times.
I remember one such trip when Emma began to travel on her own. She had caught a train from Chippenham in Wiltshire to visit her boyfriend and his family in Manchester. Unknown to her she was followed and filmed all the way to his home.

Her lawyer had quoted in the press that the insurance company of the hire company was reluctant to recognize that these where terrible injuries that called for substantial damages.

She said "I had to fight hard for Emma to receive the compensation she desperately needs for her future care and treatment".

Emma was made to feel like a criminal during these early years of her fight back to normal life. She became paranoid about who was following her, not knowing whether the person who she was sat next to and making friendly chat could in fact be one of these so called legal stalkers.

I understand that it is important that insurers are able to determine bogus claims and this can be proven by surveillance when dealing with physical injuries but a head injury is in many respects an invisible injury which carries a stigma and generally, very little understanding with regards the symptoms and effect.

A statement by the insurers said:

"As insurers we have a duty to care to all policy holders to investigate claims thoroughly. Covert surveillance is used from time to time on select cases; the use of this is strictly controlled because we are mindful of the individual's right to privacy enshrined in the Human rights act".

We were in a battle, not just for Emma's life but also her future.

This is a poem that Emma wrote that reveals what she was enduring and feeling at the time.

'Cage of court' by Emma Hamilton.   27th March 2004

The weight on my shoulders is now the heaviest yet.
Its getting bigger and bigger, darker and darker.
Suicidal thoughts.
As that is the only way to 'soften the blow' and get me out of this situation, but NO!
I want life, but my life! Not everyone else's.
All I'm doing 24:7 is;

Everything doctors, solicitors, court case, cameramen all want me to do.
Even friends and family.
I just want to be free!
All that's seen is 'The client, Miss E C Hamilton'.
As the real me seems so locked away. Maybe that's why I'm feeling so bad, as Emma is fighting so hard to get out.
Out of this 'Cage of Court'.
Putting a brave face on for everyone, but really I feel on my own.
Friend's shoulders are there for me to cry upon, but they'll just carry on with life and leave me behind.
Behind in this 'Cage of Court'.
Family's view of Emma who fought through it all and is still here to tell the story.
But do not realize....I am still fighting, and the battle still isn't over for me!
I am held a prisoner of this war, in this constant 'Cage of Court'.
I've been told and been taught, how to deal with problems from my accident.
But these problems are still coming back.
I feel I am almost running out of 'fight'.
 Getting weaker and weaker, and pushed further down.
I am so enclosed by my 'court cage', which is also holding these problems.
That's the reason why, they are raising their ugly heads. As I now can't look elsewhere. So, sometimes that's all I can see.
When I'll be released, I'll have my own space once again. To see what I want to see, and do what I want to do.

But most of all;
To be who I want to be again!!!!!

CHAPTER NINE

REHAB

It had been nearly three years since her accident and it was so hard admitting her into Residential Rehab.
The period was for an initial period of three months, she had been so positive as she regained her strength with a feeling of having a future to work towards.

The team at Collumpton Devon were very professional and the centre was well equipped. But for Emma it was like a big reminder, she was leaving the place she felt safe and loved. Now she was going back into a sheltered place of care. It was like a step back but it was absolutely necessary to establish Emma's progress and long term needs. She was surrounded by others with various levels of brain injuries and we could tell she did not want to be there.

Unfortunately this was all part of the requirement for her compensation claim, but having said that, it provided us with a full comprehensive assessment of her condition and expected long term recovery levels. We would visit her weekly for what became a pretty stressful time for Emma and ourselves.

She would endure the screams of other residents and at times those who would impose themselves on her space, like one guy with similar injuries who would often enter her room pretending to be James Bond.

We were learning about some of the complex social behavior that is common with head injuries through a combination of tests, reports, personal experience and help from God.

Her weekly routine would comprise of a day in a charity shop doing window dressing which she loved, Physiotherapy and Occupational therapy, gym and swimming. She was being continually assessed and monitored.

One of her reports read:

"Emma has difficulty coping with the emotional impact of her injury. She has a reduced ability to appreciate her own abilities, which in turn reduce her self esteem and confidence. In addition, Emma has distorted perceptions of others, resulting in low mood and poor judgment of social interactions. Emma has developed an anxiety-type thought pattern towards achievements, and as a result often resists attempts in order to avoid failure. Her fear and worry about situations reduces her ability to cope, and an avoidance pattern eventuates".

The goal for her rehab was to receive regular input from a clinical Psychologist using a cognitive behavioral therapy approach to help her to develop coping skills that will provide her with the ability to identify distorted thought patterns, challenge these and substitute them with more helpful and realistic thoughts. This was aimed at aiding in her coping with the impact of the injury and leading to an increased self-esteem and confidence.

It was noted that Emma lacked control on her moods and was leading to conflict with people around her creating increased anxiety. She would also at times be overwhelmed in busy, noisy environments".

While Emma had been wonderfully raised up and was continuing to be restored we could also see that much of her life had changed and that she had lost much of the social and cognitive skills that we all learn naturally as we are growing up.
She would need to re-learn those cognitive skills again albeit through a different process. The need for the re-learning process would take its toll causing fatigue and frustration for Emma. She would need to sleep every few hours.

Her concentration levels were very low, she loved reading but now this was not possible for any more then a few minutes. Her memory was poor but praise God that in time her memory would return. To this day she doesn't remember the accident and her time in hospital, this we think was a good thing which reduced the effects of trauma on her life.

Her friends would struggle to understand her, trying to make sense of her mood swings and subsequently feel threatened with her strange behavior. It was as if the social barriers that

govern our behavior and borders had been removed. The damage to her frontal lobe area of her brain had affected her abilities to reason and solve problems. Working through issues and conversations would often result in a stressful situation. This for her friends became a challenge and created a lot of anxiety for them.
We thank God those same friends have remained faithful friends to this day.

We felt that we had imposed this time of incarceration upon her and felt so much pain leaving her in an unnatural environment, hadn't she been through enough pain.
Pam and I would just weep as we left our daughter and drove the two hours back to Devizes.

Oh how we rejoiced when three months later we took the journey for the last time, picking her up and after thanking the staff for a fantastic job we departed for our happy journey home.

CHAPTER TEN

CARE WORKERS AT HOME

Her rehabilitation program continued at home. Emma was allocated a number of care workers or so called enablers, some of which were unable to cope with the responsibility of caring for Emma. I remember one such care worker leaving the house distraught and confused never to return.

We came to learn that the psychological effects of a head injury are very complex. Patience, understanding, perseverance, commitment and love are necessary qualities when caring for someone with a head injury.
We were learning as we went along and knew at times even our own involvement was a massive challenge for Emma. She was extremely vulnerable and we were probably over bearing and even smothering her at times. This came out of our desire to protect her and for all the family, we were on a sharp learning curve.

We had been Emma's sole carers since her return home but now three years later her life was part filled with strangers, some of which were brilliant who even forged long term friendships.

At one stage one of her friends became her carer, working through the daily activitities like cooking cleaning and planning, activities she once did as a matter of course but now needed re-training. Her life was not her own but she continued to hold onto her hope and belief that she would one day get her life back and step out again into her dreams and aspirations for the future.

Employing enablers gave us all, Pam in particular much needed times of respite especially as we had the responsibility of running a Christian school based in the church as well as my pastoral responsibilities.

Life at home was a bit of a roller coaster of emotions, working through the relational issues dealing with Emma's mood swings and at times paranoia. Sometimes a hug of love and assurance was all that was needed. We had learnt to avoid any conflict or confrontation, it was difficult and very painful so better to step back, take a deep breath, and let some time go by.

I am not an expert on these matters, the effects of head injuries or any mental illness is enormous. What we had to deal with was miniscule compared to what Emma was facing. Her life as she knew it was ripped away from her, yes she was still alive but everything else had changed. She was still the 18 year old daughter we loved but now she needed us more then ever.

Instead of letting her fly we found ourselves caring for her as a young child again. She was vulnerable, impulsive, argumentative, a fragile, and even occasionally abusive, all these things but she was still precious both to us and God. As the months rolled into years we slowly began to see the Emma we all knew returning, she was coming back, her sense of humor, her caring heart, her generosity to others all these characteristics and more, like a rose blossoming in the sunshine, she began to smile again.

She holds no bitterness in her heart, choosing rather to forgive the person who caused her to nearly lose her life.

Eph 4:31 *Let all bitterness and wrath and anger and clamor and slander be put away from you, along with all malice.^{32} Be kind to one another, tenderhearted, forgiving one another, as God in Christ forgave you.*

We choose to hate, choose to love, choose to forgive, choose to serve and what we choose to do will, in the main determine our future. Unforgiveness will foster a heart of bitterness that will rob us of our joy, our peace and our destiny, as a result we become the victims.

As we are forgiven and subsequently set free through our faith in Jesus, let us beware that we do not return to bondage due to our inability to forgive others. Forgiveness is liberating and it was accomplished through the shedding of blood on the cross by Jesus. As He has forgiven then so must we forgive others.

Ephesians1:^{7} In him we have redemption through his

blood, the forgiveness of our trespasses, according to the riches of his grace.

CHAPTER ELEVEN

BE A FIGHTER

Now Emma is a fighter and when the Psychologists and Neurological experts tell Emma she will not be able to do certain things because of her injuries then she becomes more determined to prove them wrong. Not because she is a rebel but because she believes God is greater then anything else. She also grew up with two brothers and had learnt to stand her ground and fight her corner.

Prior to her accident Emma had taken up kick boxing, mainly to get fit and fit she was. Little did she know that she would be facing the biggest fight of her life.

She was told during her time of rehab that she would never drive due to her brains inability to multi task or process multi choice situations, she now drives albeit after seven attempts to pass her test and at times frightening the life out of me. She became a familiar face in the local car paint body shop in Hadfield where she now lives. Fortunately only small dents and scratches but lots of them.

She had also been diagnosed with epilepsy and had many seizures small and large including a Grand Mal, the worse type, which caused her to be hospitalized in Manchester.

Before her accident she had met a boyfriend at Cefn Lea Christian Holiday Park in mid Wales. As the son of a pastor they had much in common. He and his family had supported her through the many stages of her recovery and after about nine years she moved near Manchester to be near him. Their relationship did not last but they remain friends.
The moving to Manchester enabled Emma to move on from the many painful memories of Devizes.

Emma no longer suffers from epilepsy she takes no medication and has been free from seizures for many years, praise God.

On a separate doctors appointment early in her rehab Emma was classified as severely disabled which qualified her for welfare support. After a period of a few years she contacted the Welfare Department and told them she did not want her disability payment.
"This does not happen", the person on the other end of the phone told her she was entitled to it and should have it. As far as Emma was concerned God was continuing to heal her and thoughts of being severely disabled, would, in her mind hold her back, someone else needier could have it.

She was told by employment experts she would never be able to work. She has retrained as a theatrical make up artist and does freelance work under her business name ECH Visuals.

This means that she is able to work on her terms, it might just be for a few hours and often it is voluntary but it provides her the outlet to be creative and productive. She has never given up, never stopped believing.

She is a fighter.

Romans 8:31 *What then shall we say to these things? If God is for us, who can be against us?* *32 He who did not spare his own Son but gave him up for us all, how will he not also with him graciously give us all things* *35 Who shall separate us from the love of Christ? Shall tribulation, or distress, or persecution, or famine, or nakedness, or danger, or sword? 36 As it is written, "For your sake we are being killed all the day long; we are regarded as sheep to be slaughtered." 37 No, in all these things we are more than conquerors through him who loved us. 38 For I am sure that neither death nor life, nor angels nor rulers, nor things present nor things to come, nor powers, 39 nor height nor depth, nor anything else in all creation, will be able to separate us from the love of God in Christ Jesus our Lord.*

She has often said she would swap every penny of her compensation to have her life back, but she has a life that she hopes will give glory to God as she witnesses and confesses that God has healed her.

You see it's the 2% that really gives him the glory.

Like the little reminder that God is still completing what He has begun, or the reminder never to forget her amazing miracle and what an incredible God we have.

Philippians 1:6 And I am sure of this, that he who began a good work in you will bring it to completion at the day of Jesus Christ.

Jesus said "Take up your cross and follow me" maybe Emma's 2% is her cross to bear every day for Jesus. Declaring that "here by the grace of God go I" and testifying, that no matter what I have been through, no matter what I am suffering, I will praise my God giving thanks to Him in all circumstances.

The apostle Paul spoke of his weakness:

2 Corinthians 11:[30] If I must boast, I will boast of the things that show my weakness.

God is looking for our humility and change of heart to praise Him even in the storms.

CHAPTER TWELVE

EMMA'S OWN WORDS

My name is Emma Hamilton, I was 18 years of age, with, thank God, the rest of my life to look forward to. I would just like to tell you how God answered the prayers of hundreds of people from around the world and here in Britain.

"All these people praying, just for me."

I had been badly injured in a car crash and doctors had told my parents they didn't expect me to live. It was thought that even if I did I would probably be severely brain damaged.

The first thing I remembered after the crash was waking up in hospital wondering why I was there. I had no remembrance of the crash at all and thought to myself that I must be in hospital having had an operation to remove my appendix.

The accident happened in September 1997. I had just finished work and decided to go out with a mate. We both got ready and had a really great time. It was soon time to go home and we were offered a lift home. Unfortunately we didn't reach home.

As far as I recall it we jumped into a friends car and off we went to bed.

I don't mean that as it sounds, but to me the car turned into a thing with wheels, very white sheets and a hard mattress.
I was later to find out that the car we were travelling in had lost control, gone through a wall and rolled over a few times. It stopped on its roof! There were three others in the car, including the driver, who came too and realized what had happened. They told me they had looked at me, wondering why I was so quiet.

They said I looked like a dummy.

Then they realized I was unconscious, I had hit my head so hard that it had knocked me out. Everyone climbed out of the car and then pulled me through the shattered windscreen and laid me on the floor.

Fortunately, a policewoman living just down the road heard the crash and rapidly came to help. She contacted all the emergency services and they arrived quickly.
I was taken to the hospital in Bath for treatment. After I had been checked over I was immediately transferred to Frenchay Hospital in Bristol. I was in a critical state and the doctors and nurses thought I wouldn't make it. Well, I had several operations, and if the doctors had followed what the medical books said about my injuries, operating on would have been a waste of time.

After several operations I fell into a coma. The general view was to wait and see what would happen. My parents were told that I would probably be brain dead or paralyzed when I woke up. Well I did return back to life, and I wasn't brain dead, or paralysed. I came out of the coma with lots of energy that I really used to fight my injuries. I was so active that I used to hit or kick the nurses and I was always trying to pull out the many tubes I had in me. I was even throwing things like pillows and teddies. Of course I didn't realize what I was doing. I was placed in a High dependency ward to see what would happen.

Unfortunately I couldn't walk and the big worry was that I would be paralysed. I couldn't stand on my own, or else I would fall over let alone walk.

After only five weeks I was able to go home; my balance was so much better that I could stand and walk on my own. I do feel bad about how everyone felt, and the worry everyone had been through, especially my family.
My parents suffered so much from anxiety and it was difficult for them to let go and put their trust in God.
When they did God began to work and take over. My accident affected many people in many different ways, but throughout it all it has spoken and shown goodness. So many people were involved.

Whilst I was ill hundreds of people got to hear about me. I was in the newspapers and the gossip of my home town of Devizes. I had so many visitors while in hospital, from a lot of people that hadn't even paid much attention to me before. People were breaking down in tears and wondering why it was happening to me. There was so much joy in folks when I returned home, and even some people thought they were seeing a ghost!!

I have never had so much attention in my life before, and I really don't know why I was in so many people's hearts. Now I'm never ignored, even by strangers. It gives me the opportunity to tell them what God has done for me.

Now I am filled with so much courage I can tell them that if God can help me:

He can deal with any problems in anyone's life.

Emma

CHAPTER THIRTEEN

TWENTY YEARS LATER

After seeing a uniformed carer with an old man who was abusively and repeatedly poking his tongue out at me, I was reminded of some unforgettable memories; How I used to be just like him...

Although the accident's court doors had finally been closed, the true 'doors' of my life had only just reopened. It was the start of my second chance.

Today I am surrounded by plenty of other things in life, but unfortunately nothing takes 'those memories' away. So whenever I am unwontedly haunted by them now, I never forget how great I am compared to back then.
I have spent over ten years settled down in the North West, now living the Mancunian way. One of the first things I did after relocating was picking up a hobby; playing a Saxophone.

Still in a rehabilitation mode, this was a great recovery task indeed. By thinking of something totally abstract to what had overpowered my mind since September 1997, it was a good 'mental breather'.

To this day whenever the unfortunate anxious feelings start playing games again with me, by concentrating more on something else, freshly clears my mind again.

Due to my mental vulnerabilities that being brain damaged has left me with, anxiety, depression, fears, and guilt, all have far more definite results on myself, IF I do not self- manage them appropriately today.

Unfortunately, I still suffer from a very unreadable and unpredictable fatigue system. I miss how previously in life I was able to know what I could bear and handle before that tiredness settled in and knowing the causes and cures for it. But now after years of trying, I still have found no patterns into my energy levels and, although with many Diabetic symptoms, I have been medically diagnosed with a 'misreading of brain signals'- a typical side effect caused from previous brain damage. Of which I have been aware through my recovery, matters other than just my energy levels had also been affected by this.

I see that difference between mental tiredness and just lack of sleep tiredness, much more obvious now. Although my general senses are not quite what they used to be (except surprisingly enough my sight was never effected), through all the difficult times of rehabilitation, I had to learn to live with all these unexpected changes of life.

So over all these years since it happened I have had to virtually re-write and adapt my whole life on total different terms than before this accident happened.

Being the equivalent of a crashed computer shutting down, and needing to reboot it with a new system and software, but in the hope that the previous data was still retrievable.

But one point of my whole being that has never changed, then and certainly will never change in my future; God.

Growing up in a great Christian family background, and known to be a perfect school girl with no bad terms or influences. Getting fully qualified at college too, and about to advance from my weekend and holiday job into the big occupational world of adults.

So, when I almost lost my life that night everything had dramatically been turned upside down, effecting myself and all my surrounding family and friends back then and up to the present day now. Now in hope I always live up to my new status I had been awarded since that time of life changing happenings;

A true walking miracle.

From vaguely remembering my first hospital release. The surprisingly shocked looks worn on many faces, after realising who it was they could now see walking down my local High street again. They had all heard of the major disruptive events and results, with a local presumption I was dead. Entering into a room to see another medical person who will be updating my own health status and records.
But with a puzzled look on the Doctor's face and needing to double check with the nurse that they had the right paperwork in front of them. After asking for my confirmation of my name again, "something else was definitely working with you" was told.

Since then, on hearing several times again similar statements from others also working in the medical world, has made that quote an unforgettable statement and great reminder of who I owe so much thanks to; God.

Being a great reminder to others that their requests were definitely not ignored too and sometimes having to say nothing, keeps me encouraged to use my story of miraculous success to help out others when needed. No matter what had happened "back then" I was determined to use my second chance's greatest prospects, and getting back onto the normal road of life again was my main goal.

After finally passing my driving test I went back into education and became a qualified (and now experienced) freelance Media Makeup Artist. Running my own life again, was exactly what I had wanted, after experiencing such major factors of life; I had had no real personal control over before.

All the care and love both family and friends had given to me in my recovery, will never be forgotten. But it was still down to me how much recovery my life would actually see, and then be seen by others.

Starting from that day, when my motionless body lay surrounded by many tears and fears of what would be happening to me next..........my little finger had suddenly twitched.
This was my first sign of true life again, the start of my "rollercoaster ride of recovery" and the surprisingly and unpredictable results to many others.

I believe I am still here for a reason, so I continue to put my trust in Him as to what will happen next.

Only God knows.

Emma

Emma is now married and hoping to start a family. Many of her life skills have returned such as cooking, drawing and home making, she is a planner and a motivator. She is active in her local church teaching Sunday school to the children. She has even learnt to play the saxophone and plays it pretty good. and against the odds can even read music. She has travelled and has many friends many of which have stood by her throughout the years of her recovery.

Her faith is strong as she continually gives thanks to God for her healing.

She still has to work through the two percent bit, but she has her life, a life that is a testimony of Gods amazing love and healing power.

KEEP LOOKING UP

Prayer:

If you feel that Emma's story has spoken to you concerning your need to know God more or maybe you want to trust Him more during the many challenges that you will face in the future, then take a few moments to pray this prayer, being assured that He will hear your prayer:

Heavenly Father, thank you for sending your Son Jesus into the world to die for me as my Saviour.
I believe and receive your healing and restoration for my life.
Thank you Lord that you know every thing about me and you have the answer to every situation and challenge that I am going through right now and including those that I will face in the future.
I believe The Holy Spirit will guide, strengthen and help me in all circumstances.
My prayer is that through my life, You will be glorified and that You will mold me as a child of God to be an effective witness for You in this world. Amen

Psalms 23

The LORD Is My Shepherd.

The LORD is my shepherd; I shall not want.
He makes me lie down in green pastures. He leads me beside still waters.
He restores my soul. He leads me in paths of righteousness for his name's sake.
Even though I walk through the valley of the shadow of death, I will fear no evil, for you are with me; your rod and your staff, they comfort me.
You prepare a table before me in the presence of my enemies; you anoint my head with oil; my cup overflows.
Surely goodness and mercy shall follow me all the days of my life, and I shall dwell in the house of the LORD forever.

Pastor David Hamilton can be contacted by email on:

davepamham@gmail.com

Scripture translation used: English Standard Version.